Echoes
in the
Abyss

Hymns of Loss & Restoration in an Existential Disarray

Maneesh

BLUEROSE PUBLISHERS
India | U.K.

Copyright © Maneesh 2024

All rights reserved by author. No part of this publication may be reproduced, stored in a retrieval system or transmitted in any form or by any means, electronic, mechanical, photocopying, recording or otherwise, without the prior permission of the author. Although every precaution has been taken to verify the accuracy of the information contained herein, the publisher assumes no responsibility for any errors or omissions. No liability is assumed for damages that may result from the use of information contained within.

BlueRose Publishers takes no responsibility for any damages, losses, or liabilities that may arise from the use or misuse of the information, products, or services provided in this publication.

For permissions requests or inquiries regarding this publication, please contact:

BLUEROSE PUBLISHERS
www.BlueRoseONE.com
info@bluerosepublishers.com
+91 8882 898 898
+4407342408967

ISBN: 978-93-6452-875-7

Cover design: Shivam
Typesetting: Namrata Saini

First Edition: October 2024

To

Daddy & Mummy

ततश्चानुदिनं धर्मः सत्यं शौचं क्षमा दया ।
कालेन बलिना राजन् नङ्क्ष्यत्यायुर्बलं स्मृतिः ॥

(श्रीमद्भागवतपुराणम्/स्कन्धः 12/अध्यायः 2/ श्लोक 01)

In the Kaliyuga era, attributes such as religion, truthfulness, cleanliness, tolerance, kindness, lifespan, physical strength, and memory will gradually decline with each passing day.

अनावृष्ट्या विनङ्क्ष्यन्ति दुर्भिक्षकरपीडिताः
शीतवातातपप्रावृड् हिमैरन्योन्यतः प्रजाः ॥

(श्रीमद्भागवतपुराणम्/स्कन्धः 12/अध्यायः 2/ श्लोक 10)

In Kaliyuga, the absence of rain will result in drought. Additionally, there will be times of intense cold and times of extreme heat. At times, there will be a storm, and at others, a flood will occur. These circumstances will trouble people and lead to their downfall.

Contents

Preface vii

Acknowledgement xi

I The Verses 1

What is it to be? 3

Haunted 5

The Last Day 7

When 'They' Met 'Them' 10

Echoes in the Abyss 13

Hollowness 15

Democracy 17

Silenced, Not Dead Though! 19

The Alchemists of Betrayal 21

The Tempters' Tribunal 23

Leonidas Calvus 27

The Modern Masquerade 30

The Last Leaf 34

Chiaroscuro 37

Traced and Catalogued 40

Where Justice Fears To Tread 42

A World Reborn 44

Freed From 'Freedom' 47

Dreamscape of Illusions 50

Misunderstood 52

The Greyscale 54

Caged 56

Wrecked and Lost 57

Tinkling of Terror 59

#(Hashtag)Love 62

II *The Eternal Embrace* 65

The Prologue 67

Canto 1: The Fateful Meeting 70

Canto 2: The Enchanted Bond 73

Canto 3: The Dark Prophecy 76

Canto 4: The Quest for the Amulet 81

Canto 5: The Betrayal 86

Canto 6: The Reclaimed Realm 91

Canto 7: The Festival of Unity 94

Canto 8: The Shadows Return 97

Canto 9: The Last Confrontation 100

Canto 10: The Eternal Embrace 103

Preface

In the midst of a world increasingly overshadowed by despair, hopelessness, and loss, an era marked by rapid change, constant uncertainty, and profound disillusionment, we often find ourselves grappling with the weight of existence itself. It is quite natural to find ourselves confronting the questions of existence. This book of poems emerges from a place of profound contemplation, grappling with the existential crisis that seems to loom over our collective consciousness. As we navigate a world fraught with despair, hopelessness, and loss, these poems offer a reflective and intimate exploration of the human condition. The poems in this collection are born from the depths of this existential struggle, reflecting the silent battles fought within the human spirit when confronted with a seemingly indifferent universe.

Each verse is a fragment of the soul's search for meaning amid the disarray of modern life. The language of these poems is raw and unfiltered, echoing the existential questions that haunt us—about purpose, identity, and the essence of being. They offer no easy answers but instead serve as a mirror to our collective anguish and introspection.

These verses are not crafted out of detachment but out of a deep, visceral engagement with the trials that shape our reality. They speak to the shadows that linger in the corners of our minds and the silent grief that pervades our lives. They are a testament to the disquieting recognition that our existence can often feel like a fragile thread suspended in an indifferent universe.

Existentialism posits that meaning is not handed to us by the world but is something we must each seek and create in the face of a seemingly meaningless cosmos. This collection does not offer simplistic answers or consolatory rhetoric but delves into the raw and often uncomfortable truths about the nature of our being. The language used is intentionally stark, aiming to resonate with the authenticity of our deepest fears and longings. It reflects the internal and external chaos that many of us experience but find difficult to articulate.

The poems are not just isolated musings but a continuum of existential reflection. Each piece stands as a solitary inquiry while also contributing to a broader narrative about the human struggle with meaning. You will find within these lines an examination of the fundamental questions: What is our place in a world that seems so indifferent? How do we reconcile the inevitable experiences of loss and sorrow with our desire for purpose and connection? Through these verses, I hope to create a space where readers can confront their own existential dilemmas. This book is an invitation to engage with the uncertainties and complexities of our existence. It is a space where discomfort and melancholy are acknowledged and embraced, not as final states but as part of the ongoing process of seeking and understanding.

Ultimately, the aim of this collection is not to offer definitive solutions but to underscore the shared human experience of grappling with profound questions. By giving voice to these uncertainties and reflections, I hope to offer a sense of companionship in the struggle, a reminder that we are not alone in our quest for meaning. This book is not merely an exploration of sorrow, but a testament to the resilience of the human heart. Through its pages, I invite you to embark on a journey through the shadows of existence, to confront your own fears and uncertainties, and to find solace in the shared experience of our collective struggle. In the end, perhaps these words will provide not just an acknowledgment of our despair, but a glimmer of hope that, despite everything, the quest for understanding and connection endures.

May these poems serve as a mirror to your own existential reflections and provide a measure of solace in the knowledge that our search for understanding is both deeply personal and universally human. In the echo of these verses, may you find a resonance with your own experiences and perhaps a glimmer of hope in the shared journey through the labyrinth of existence.

Maneesh

Acknowledgement

This book of poems is the culmination of not just my own efforts, but the unwavering support and encouragement of those who have been pillars of strength. This has been an intensely personal journey, and it is with deep gratitude that I acknowledge those who have supported and inspired me along the way.

Daddy and Mummy, your boundless love and encouragement have been the foundation upon which this work rests. Your belief in my abilities has been a source of immense strength, and your unwavering support has guided me through moments of doubt. Thank you for nurturing my dreams and for being my steadfast supporters.

Raju and Neha, you both have been constant motivation in the moments of acute personal and emotional crisis. Raju, your insightful conversations have sparked new ideas and perspectives. And Neha, your encouragement has helped me in finding my roots again as a student of literature. Thank you both for being a source of light during the darkest moments of this journey. I am deeply grateful for your presence and support.

Pragya, when you came into life, I had already lost all hopes. But your love, patience, and understanding, have been the greatest anchors to my drowning hopes. Your unwavering belief in my work and your thoughtful support have been crucial to this book's creation.

Mishka and Shubhi, even though just kids, your presence has brought an unparalleled joy and inspiration to my life. The innocence and wonder you bring into our lives have deeply influenced my writing. It is just because of you both, my sweethearts, that my verses take an occasional turn to life and hope.

To my Teachers Dr. Professor Anita Singh and Dr. Professor Bani Brat Mahanta, I owe all my life and insight (whatever little I do have). You two are my Muse when I think of writing. Your guidance and wisdom have profoundly shaped my understanding and approach to this work. Your guidance and constructive critiques have been pivotal in the development of these poems. Your support and understanding have provided me with the tools to explore and express my thoughts more deeply. The knowledge and wisdom you have shared have greatly enriched this work.

Each of you has contributed in unique and profound ways, and your support has been crucial in bringing this collection to fruition. Thank you for being part of this journey and for helping me give voice to the complex and often difficult themes explored within these pages.

Maneesh

I

The Verses

What is it to be?

In the dark,
A silence curls around me,
A shroud of unknowing;
Each breath,
A fragile testament to existence,
Each heartbeat,
A question unanswered.

I wander through the void,
An echo among echoes,
Seeking meaning in the abyss,
Where stars are nothing,
But specks of lost light.

The cosmos,
Indifferent and vast,
Spreads out
Like an infinite tapestry,
Each thread,
A silent whisper of dreams
Dissolved into dust.

Time folds in on itself,
A Möbius strip of moments
Where yesterday,
Bleeds into tomorrow,

And in every second lies both
A beginning and an end.

I search for a purpose;
A whisper of reason,
In the deafening roar of nothingness,
Yet find only shadows,
Shifting and elusive.

Existence is an enigma
Wrapped in paradox,
A dance of illusions,
Where certainties dissolve
Like morning mist,
And truth remains
A phantom in the dark.

What is it to be?
To be a flicker of awareness
In a boundless expanse
Of silence and stars?

The question hangs heavy,
A leaden weight upon my soul,
And in its gravity,
I am both,
The anchor and the driftwood,
Rooted in uncertainty,
Adrift in the void.

Haunted

In this new dawn where steel and glass conspire,
The city's breath is heavy with despair.
We tread on paths of data, wires, screens,
Yet feel the weight of ages in our bones.

The echoes of tomorrow haunt our steps,
With whispers of a future dark and cold,
A world where dreams are shadows, lost and faint,
And hope, a fleeting glimpse through shattered glass.

Each day we build our lives on shifting sand,
Constructing spires of progress, blind to fall,
While spectres of the future loom above,
Their silent wails an endless, creeping dread.

In this machine, our essence wears thin threads,
And though we strive for meaning in the noise,
The distant dark is all that fills our eyes—
A tale of what might come, a tale of loss.

We grasp for purpose in the restless void,
And question if our dreams are but a curse,
Haunting us with visions of our own demise,
And leave us staring at the sky in vain.

Yet still we walk, our shadows cast ahead,
In search of light within the shadowed night,
For though the future looms with veiled intent,
Our hearts persist, defying fate's dark hand.

The Last Day

I wake, an echo in the dim silence,
feeling the pull of an invisible gravity
that tugs me toward the edge of everything.
The morning light, a sullen whisper
through the curtained windows,
paints the room in shades of regret.

Each breath is a borrowed moment,
each step an echo of despair
through the emptiness of my apartment.
The walls, stripped bare of hope,
stand silent witnesses
to a life that slipped away unnoticed.

I force myself to the kitchen,
where cold cereal and faded dreams
lie side by side, a sad parody of nourishment.
The taste, a bitter reminder
of the hollow spaces where joy used to reside,
mingles with the lingering shadow of inevitability.

The city outside thrums with life,
a relentless, vibrant pulse
that feels both foreign and mocking.
I drift among the living,
a ghost in a world that turns,
unconcerned by the weight of my departure.

In the park, I find solace
among leafless trees that seem to understand,
their silence a reflection of my own.
The sky above is an indifferent expanse,
clouds drifting like thoughts
I can no longer grasp or articulate.

As dusk settles, I return to the sanctuary
of my forsaken space,
where the shadows grow long and deep,
consuming fragments of a past
that no longer matters.
The finality of it all wraps around me
like a heavy, suffocating blanket.

I write a note—few words,
more to soothe my restless spirit
than to communicate anything.
A last whisper into the void,
offering a fragment of what once was,
before the final silence.

In the deepening night,
with the weight of my decision
settling over me like a shroud,
I close my eyes,
letting the darkness
claim me as its own.

There is no grand departure,
just the quiet end
of a day that fades
into nothingness.

When 'They' Met 'Them'

In the shadowed expanse where night folds day,
Two figures drift in a realm unseen,
Odysseus, draped in time's decay,
And Ulysses, lost where gods convene.

Their paths entwine in twilight's haze,
Where myths and modern doubts collide,
In search of meaning through endless days,
And weary souls in fate abide.

Amidst the haze of barren land,
Two men await in tattered grace,
Lucky's hope held by trembling hand,
And Pozzo's pride, a waning face.

Odysseus, with eyes of sea-worn blue,
Approaches with a mystic stride,
While Ulysses, pondering and rue,
Observes with thought, a cosmic guide.

"Behold," proclaims the ancient seer,
"Our quest is ending, shadows clear,
We bring the light that you have sought,
Your wait for Godot's end is brought."
Pozzo's eyes, a flicker faint,
Mingle doubt with hope so raw,

"Speak more of this," his voice a plaint,
"Is fate so fragile, or just a flaw?"

Lucky's gaze, a hollow stare,
Reflects the void of waiting long,
"What truth lies here, in air so bare?
What melody can mend our song?"

Ulysses smiles, a silent jest,
"We drift like dust through time's own weave,
The gods are gone, yet we invest
In shadows only we conceive."

Odysseus, with heavy sigh,
Unfolds the tales of trial and woe,
"We sailed through storms and parted sky,
To find that truth is what we sow."

"In every journey," Ulysses said,
"The end is not what we pursue,
But in each step, our spirits led,
The Godot we seek is born anew."

Pozzo, gripped by shifting thoughts,
Finds solace in their cryptic lore,
His fears, like echoes, softly caught,
In wisdom's grasp, he feels restored.

Lucky, though, remains unspoke,
His mind a labyrinth of doubt,
Yet in their words, a glimmer woke,
A hope that somehow still devout.

The figures fade into the mist,
Odysseus and Ulysses gone,
Yet in their wake, a truth persists,
The quest for meaning carries on.

So here they wait in barren place,
Not for a saviour, but the dawn,
In every pause, a fleeting grace,
And in their hearts, a truth reborn.

For in the waiting, in the night,
The quest itself becomes the key,
In every search, the endless fight,
To shape the world, to truly see.

Echoes in the Abyss

In the dim-lit corridors of your intent,
I am a ghost, my voice swallowed by the dark,
Reaching out from the abyss of your cruelty.

Did you think the marrow of my spirit
Was a hollow vessel, easily shattered?
Did you believe my heart,
A fragile bird, would bend to your madness,
That my dreams, so tender, would wither
Beneath the weight of your brutality?

In the chill of that night,
I was a constellation unseen,
My life a tapestry unravelling
Under the cruel seam of your hands.
How did you not see?
How could you not grasp the truth
That every touch you forced
Was a theft of light, a stain upon humanity?

Did you think I was a mere silhouette,
A shadow on your path of depravity?
Or did the madness of your mind
Whisper lies, painting me as less than flesh,
Less than the cosmos of wonder
That was torn from me?

Why did you carve violence into the tapestry
Of my existence? What twisted dreams
Drove you to sever my voice from my body,
To drown my cries in the still, cold silence?
What madness, what darkness,
Could feed on such innocent hope?

Do you see now, in the lightless prison
Of your own making, the monument of my anguish?
Haven't the echoes of my agony
Become your only companions,
As my spirit, unyielding,
Haunts the corridors of your soul,
A testament to the violence you wrought?

And still, through the rage and the sorrow,
Through the gaping chasm of my lost life,
My wonder remains—
Not for the cruelty you embraced,
But for the resilience that survives,
A whisper against the chaos,
A flame that will not be extinguished.

Hollowness

In the mosaic of daily life,
each piece a glint of fleeting hope,
we wander through a landscape of echoes,
where conversations scatter like leaves in wind—
voices rising, falling, dissolved
into the ether of what was promised and left behind.

The air crackles with the static of grand speeches,
politicians sculpting illusions
from thin air and grand gestures,
while the pulse of reality beats on,
unseen, unheeded, a silent drum
beneath the parade of empty platitudes.

Ethics, once a lighthouse in stormy seas,
now wavers on a horizon of shifting tides,
its beacon dimmed by the fog of compromise,
a lighthouse reduced to a flicker
of what might have been, swaying
to the rhythm of convenience and self.

Academia's grand halls, once beacons of truth,
now echo with the clamour of empty accolades,
knowledge a commodity wrapped in bright covers,
its essence diluted in the pursuit
of accolades and transient fame,
leaving minds adrift in a sea of borrowed ideas.

In the realm of feeling, we are paper-thin,
fragile vessels drifting in the turbulent sea
of fleeting connections and digital embraces,
where hearts are pulled in endless loops,
seeking warmth in the cold light of screens,
finding only reflections of themselves
staring back, hollowed and unfulfilled.

Here, amidst this vast, echoing stage,
we tread carefully, our steps light and tentative,
navigating the void where meaning should reside,
each moment a whisper of what could be
if only the surface weren't so thin,
and the depths weren't so obscured
by the relentless, empty light of day.

Democracy

In the grand bazaar of democracy,
where the stalls glitter with promises,
a parade of opulence waltzes
to the tune of a thousand empty promises.

Here, the poor are the props in a grand show,
their lives mere background noise
as the rich make deals behind velvet curtains,
clinking glasses in the haze of cigars.

The politicians, painted in vivid hues,
play their roles like seasoned actors,
smiling with gold-plated teeth,
while the poor dance for scraps.

Banners wave with slogans of change,
but beneath them, the streets remain the same,
filled with the echoes of a system
that serves its masters with a grin.

Votes are the currency of this masquerade,
purchased with a nod and a handshake,
and the ballot boxes—ancient relics
in this theatre of the absurd—overflow.

From the marble halls of power
to the dust-choked corners of the slums,
a chain of command links wealth and influence,
each link polished with the sheen of corruption.

Here, the rich are the patrons,
the poor, their silent chorus,
and democracy—an elegant charade,
a well-dressed pimp of the prosperous.

And in this carnival of exploitation,
the sound of freedom rings hollow,
echoing off the opulent walls,
while the masses, in their silent desperation,
wait for a note of truth to break the silence.

Silenced, Not Dead Though!

In the grand theatre of shadows,
Where gilded masks obscure the truth,
The world's great puppeteers dance,
Strings of silence woven through their fingers.

Voices, once like storm-tossed seas,
Now lie still, a pond's glassy surface
Under the weight of a leaden sky,
Where even echoes fear to tread.

Mountains of lament, crumbling in silence,
Unheard by the earthen gods
Who sip their ambrosia from crystal chalices,
Blissfully unaware of the fissures
Beneath their gilded palace floors.

The winds of anguish blow,
But their gusts are caught
In cages of gold and iron,
Where they flutter, mute and broken,
Like birds with clipped wings.

In the dim chambers of power,
A chorus of dreams is stifled,
A great celestial choir rendered mute
By the velvet of oppression,
As constellations blink out, one by one.

Through the iron gate of sovereignty,
Truths are swallowed like dark stars
Into an abyss that swallows light,
And cries are but whispers lost
In the cacophony of control.

Yet, beneath the weight of these silences,
A faint rhythm pulses,
A heartbeat of defiance,
That murmurs softly against the granite walls,
Waiting for a crack, a fracture,
Where light may yet seep through.

The Alchemists of Betrayal

In gilded halls where whispers dance,
The opportunists convene,
Their tongues laced with treachery,
Sacrificing truth on the altar of expedience.

They pour poison into the chalice of justice,
Turning rapes and murders into mere footnotes
In their manuscripts of deceit.
Like architects of an abyss,
They sketch blueprints for a world
Where agony is trivialized,
Where the screams of the violated
Are drowned in a sea of political noise.

In the courtrooms of corruption,
Their arguments are threads of silk
Woven with the filth of compromise,
They dress crimes in the rags of ambiguity,
Seeking to soften the edge of horror
With the balm of convenience.

Watch as they craft excuses,
Delicately framing cruelty in the guise of error,
Proclaiming that the bloodshed is but
A shadow in the light of their expediency,
Their insatiable hunger for power
Trampling over the shattered bones of justice.

They are the alchemists of dishonour,
Transmuting moral outrage into political gain,
Playing with the lives of the innocent
Like pieces on a chessboard,
Moving pieces that do not bleed
But only serve to pad their coffers.

The murmurs of the oppressed
Echo through their vaulted chambers,
But to their ears, it is the din of an inconvenience,
An uninvited guest
To their grand masquerade.

We shall not let them redefine
The crimes that sear the soul,
Nor allow their diluted language
To paint horror with the brush of negligence.
For in the end,
It is not just justice they betray,
But the very essence of our shared humanity.

The Tempters' Tribunal

In the cosmic courtroom of divine discontent,
Where the golden calf still trots unrepentant,
Satan and Beelzebub, fallen from their fiery heights,
Devised a curious conspiracy—
A tale of trickster and tempter,
Slouched in the blackened recesses of their thrones.

"Hear, O Heaven," Satan proclaimed,
"for we have wandered through the realms of men,
Through gardens that rot with ambition,
And heard their wails of weary worship."

Beelzebub, the flies' king,
Crowned in stench and brimstone,
Buzzed in agreement,
"Indeed, Satan, these creatures of dust and desire,
Find themselves both blessed and burdened,
Knowing not their iniquity from their redemption."

They bemoaned their failures,
As every serpent does, grumbling beneath the surface,
For even infernal architects
Must face the creeping apocalypse of absurdity.
The accusations of sinfulness resounded,
More from boredom than from malignity.
"Shall we, O Beelzebub,

Take recourse to the grand architect of everything,
To plead our case against these men,
Whose petty prayers and misplaced piety
Mock the darkness with every dawn?"

Beelzebub buzzed with a sinister glee,
"Yes, let us ascend the firmament,
Clad in shadows and filth,
To petition the One who cast us down."

And so they trudged,
Through the chasms of celestial bureaucracy,
Bearing their bribes of ash and malcontent,
To the pearly gates where divine adjudication
Lay heavy and indifferent.

"O Great Architect!" they cried,
"Behold our plight,
For these men are truly insolent,
And we are yet unsung."

The Almighty, resplendent and aloof,
Surveyed the chaos, rolling eyes,
Peering through heavenly windows of burnished gold,
Pondered the absurdity of their appeal.

"Do you bring complaints of mankind,
As though they were mere brambles
In the garden of celestial order?"
Satan, now adorned in righteousness,

Spoke with pompous indignation,
"Indeed, O Lord, they wallow in ignorance,
With vainglorious prayers and faith in miracles,
While we, the architects of chaos,
Are left to ponder our lost prestige."

Beelzebub buzzed a droning anthem,
"Shall we not be granted respite,
From these mortal follies and frantic fancies?"

God, in eternal patience,
With a flicker of omnipotent weariness,
Replied with a voice like thunder and silent rain,
"Dost thou know, O Tempters,
That the lament of mankind is thine own creation,
A reflection of the chaos thou dost nurture?"

The cosmos chuckled in divine orchestration,
As stars twinkled in mockery,
And the universe, in its infinite jest,
Waved them away, unperturbed.

"Begone, ye heralds of discontent,
For the spectacle of humanity is a play,
Where the lines are penned by thy own hand.
To complain of the script is to wrestle with shadows."

And so they descended,
Back to the sulphurous depths,
Left to their own infernal devices,
Grumbling and scuttling,
To rebuild their rancour
With the detritus of mortal folly.

Thus ends the tale of Satan and Beelzebub,
Seeking a celestial reprieve,
Found only in their own mirthless misery,
As they shuffle the deck of despair,
In a game eternally stacked against them.

Leonidas Calvus

In the fractured landscape of the new epoch,
Where the dream of steel cities meets the pulse of machine life,
There emerges an unsung figure, sculpted in the dust of forgotten legends:
Leonidas Calvus, a name both herald and harbinger,
Born from the forges of a silicon age.

He strides past the gleaming facades of innovation,
His shadow a tapestry of contradictions,
Draped in the very fabric of the age he dares to mend,
A paradox of the new order's shape and sheen.
He wears no crown, but his presence is a scepter
In the court of fractured ideals.

Calvus, with eyes like those ancient orbs
That once read the stars, now scrutinizes
The tangled algorithms and rusted promises
Of a world built on the ashes of its own hubris.
Not a hero in the truest sense,
But a maestro of discord and disillusionment,
A whisper against the roar of progress's fanfare.

His cloak is not woven from the threads of virtue,
But from the tattered remnants of every broken dream,
And he wields no sword of righteousness,

Only the pen of subversion and the dialectic of truth.
He is a paradox—a Prometheus shackled
By the very fire he seeks to ignite.

Where the world spins in its relentless dance of zeros and ones,
Calvus dances a waltz of dissent,
Refracting the light of the old gods through lenses
Cracked by the weight of modernity's glare.
He is the reflection of shadows in the mirror's edge,
The murmur of rebellion in the clamour of conformity.

He takes no part in the parades of empty triumphs,
Nor does he sit at the high tables of the great and the good,
But in the dim alleys where the neon's hum
Sings of forgotten promises, he sows seeds of change,
Each word a revolutionary act,
Each gesture a testament to the power of the unspoken.

Calvus rides not on chariots, but on the currents of discontent,
His banner the flag of those cast aside,
A herald for the whispers of the silenced,
The cries of the unseen in the theatre of the grand.
His revolution is not one of bloody conquest,
But of quiet reformation,
A patient architect of the world's rebirth.
In the corridors of power and the silos of wealth,

He stands as a lone echo against the thunderous applause
Of a world drunk on its own spectacle.
His legacy will not be one of heroic grandeur,
But of a recalibrated compass,
Pointing towards a horizon forged in the fires of realignment.

Leonidas Calvus, the name itself a blend
Of ancient valour and modern discontent,
Crafts the future from the shards of the present,
Championing not the age of glory,
But the silent revolution of the everyday.

In the pages of history, he may not inscribe
His name in letters of gold,
But in the whispers of the future,
His influence will be felt in the quiet
Rebirth of a world more just,
More aware,
More human.

The Modern Masquerade

In fair Verona's realm of yore,
Where once did love's grand passions soar,
Behold, where hearts did weave their spell
And Cupid's arrows struck so well,
Now here we stand, in modern guise,
Where love's a tweet or quick replies,
And Romeo, with Juliet,
Wears a guise most counterfeit.

On shores of Adige, long ago,
Where love did once its ardour show,
There bloomed a tale of rapture bright,
'neath stars that shone with pure delight.
But now, this tale from yesteryears,
Where lovers' vows brought joyful tears,
Transforms to shadows, faint and thin,
As modern hearts find naught within.

Behold, where once sweet Romeo wept,
And Juliet in silence kept
Her heart alight with fervent flame,
In courts of love and timeless name,
Now rests a scene both trite and tame,
Where hearts are lost in fleeting game.
For modern loves, like fickle birds,
Seek only tweets and shallow words.

O Juliet! thy love's true grace,
Now hides behind a hollow face.
And my Love! To you I vow,
A thousand hearts on "Swipe Right" now,
O Romeo! Thou art half of what
Thy lovely name once did exalt,
And my Love! thy gaze so fleet,
Is lost within a meme and tweet.

Once did their eyes, with ardent fire,
Set hearts alight with pure desire,
Yet now, in screens' eternal glow,
No more do ardent passions show.
No longer do they yearn in vain,
For love's deep truths or heart's true pain,
But rather scroll through endless feeds,
And satisfy their transient needs.

The balcony, a stage so grand,
Where once did lovers' hearts expand,
Now hosts a screen with scroll and swipe,
Where texts are traded with a type.
No more do whispered oaths suffice,
Nor sonnets penned in moon's soft light,
But rather hearts, with faces cold,
Find fleeting joy in gestures sold.

The theatre, a quaint affair,
Replaced by "Likes" and stifled air,
For in this age of fleeting fun,
Where texts and emojis swiftly run,
Love's grandeur shrinks to snippets brief,
Where sentiment is but a leaf
That rustles in the winds of change,
In virtual realms so vast, so strange.

Once tragic fate, with swords and woe,
Now calls forth clicks and status quo,
Where hearts are tossed in digital seas,
And longing fades like autumn leaves.
No longer do the lovers pine,
For instant gratification's shrine,
Where every vow is laced with snark,
And passion's light grows faint and dark.

How strange it is, this modern plight,
Where feelings freeze in digital night,
And Romeo, with thumbs that dance,
No longer seeks love's true romance.
He's lost amidst the "likes" and "shares,"
And Juliet's heart, though still she cares,
Now wanders through a sea of memes,
Where love's true depth is lost in dreams.

Oh, let us muse on this decay,
Where sentiment has gone astray,
And wonder how the hearts that beat
With passion's fervour, once so sweet,
Have turned to vapid, quick delights,
And lost their way in shallow flights.
For in this world of instant gain,
True love's deep bonds seem quite inane.

O Romeo! O Juliet!
To what strange fate are ye beget?
Not in Verona's ancient night,
But in a world of shallow plight,
Where love's deep currents swift do die,
Beneath the weight of one more lie.
So let us toast to love's demise,
In modern days of thin disguise.

The Last Leaf

In the barren wood, where shadows lean,
And frost sharpens the breath of the day,
There stands, amid the skeletal limbs,
A solitary leaf, clinging with a resolve
As old as the earth and the sky.

It quivers in the whispering wind,
A lone emerald among the greyed veins
Of ancient trees, their bark like cracked parchment,
Secrets scrawled in the language of time.
The leaf, though frail, holds steadfast,
A sentinel of verdure in a sea of decay.

Winter's breath is a frostbitten hymn,
Sung by the hollow bones of the forest,
A dirge for life's fragile splendour
Where every branch is an elegy
And every sigh is the echo of eternity.

Yet, the leaf, defiant in its fragile grace,
Dreams the dreams of the ancients,
Of sunlight piercing through the cold shrouds,
Of spring's tender whisper that wakes
The world from its sepulchral sleep.
It is not mere green, but a whisper
Of what was and what might yet be,

A hint of Eden in the bleak expanse,
A promise wrought in chlorophyll,
Carved by the same hands that shape
The arc of constellations and the sigh of seas.

In the leaf's delicate veins, histories dance—
From the murmurs of the early dawn
To the echoes of summer's symphony,
A tapestry woven in the loom of hope,
Spun by the dreamers of yore.

Its stubborn pulse is a testimony,
A script etched in the language of survival,
Saying, amidst the silence of a world bereft,
That even as all seems lost,
There remains a single, steadfast thread
Binding the heart to the promise of return.

For in the leaf's trembling form,
One finds not just the beauty of resistance,
But the quiet strength of a singular dream
That refuses to dissolve into the cold wind,
That waits, patiently, for the rebirth
Of the world that will follow the frost.

And so, in the barren wood, amid the sighs
Of ancient giants and the creeping chill,
This last leaf, trembling but alive,
Stands as a beacon, a green spark
In the enveloping grey, a reminder
That even in the coldest, darkest times,
The smallest light can kindle the dawn.

Chiaroscuro

In the shady greys of the 21st century,
where shadows stretch like frayed fabric
over fractured landscapes,
our lives, pixels in a vast, digital mosaic,
flicker with dissonant rhythms.

We wander through cities
that hum with the electric pulse of progress,
yet echo with an ancient loneliness,
each street a corridor of mirages,
each face a mask of hollowed dreams.

Skyscrapers rise, sharp as broken teeth,
their glassy skins reflecting
the empty skies, like shattered promises.
Concrete veins snake through our existence,
carrying the lifeblood of data,
while the air thickens with static,
and the silence between the transmissions
deepens into a chasm.

In the hum of our devices,
a cacophony of voices,
we seek solace in a thousand scattered fragments—
memes and soundbites, likes and shares,
the currency of validation
in a world where touch has turned to screen.

We are soldiers of the infinite scroll,
trapped in the loop of now and not quite,
our memories stored in clouded archives,
while the present evaporates like mist,
leaving only the spectral echoes of a past
that no longer aligns with the present's pulse.

Nations become pixels of discord,
unravelled borders drawn anew
by algorithms and invisible hands,
as we watch from the periphery,
our connections stretched thin
across bandwidths and time zones,
our common threads frayed and torn.

Nature's slow retreat
paints the backdrop with sombre hues,
its rhythms disrupted, its creatures
lost in the haze of extinction's toll,
while we chase the flickering light
of screens that cannot grasp
the weight of the world outside.

And in the heart of this disarray,
we still search for meaning
in the bits and bytes of a disenchanted age,
where each truth is relative,
and each dream, a fragile whisper
in the void of our collective memory.

Yet amidst the shattering,
there are moments of quiet rebellion—
a single hand reaching out
through the electric haze,
a voice rising against the noise,
a spark of humanity
in the machine's cold embrace.

We are fragments and whole,
lost and found in the dark,
a paradox of existence,
seeking connection in the void,
struggling to piece together
the shards of a reality
that has slipped through
our grasping fingers, yet still
tells the story of who we are.

In this 21st-century *chiaroscuro*,
where the night seems endless
and the dawn perpetually deferred,
we navigate the labyrinth
of our own making,
each step a testament
to the resilience of the human spirit,
each breath a defiant whisper
against the encroaching silence.

Traced and Catalogued

In this century of whispers and steel,
our shadows shrink in the glow of screens,
where eyes and ears, unseen but constant,
hunger for fragments of our lives.

Walls have become mere suggestions,
privacy a fading concept,
as we weave our days in digital threads,
each moment laid bare for scrutiny.

The hum of data flows through the air,
invisible networks binding us
in webs of electric desire,
our footsteps traced, our voices catalogued.

We speak into the void,
believing in the freedom of our words,
yet each utterance is a seed,
planted in the fertile ground of algorithms.

How often do we ponder
the silent observers, the passive eyes,
their gaze a constant weight
upon the subtle contours of our lives?

The curtain between self and world
is now a gauzy veil,
thin and fragile,
fluttering in the breeze of relentless observation.

And as we navigate this intricate maze,
do we forget what it means
to be unseen, unheard,
to find solace in the embrace of anonymity?

In this era where every whisper
is archived, analyzed, and projected,
we seek a sanctuary,
a corner of our existence untouched,
a place where the clamour of surveillance fades,
and the essence of our being
can breathe freely once more.

Where Justice Fears To Tread

In a world where the gavel's echo is swallowed by a void,
And justice is a shadow of gold,
The judge in every man awakens,
Glaring with hunger through cracked facades.

Here, morality's scales are as brittle as glass,
And law, once a sacred iron, is twisted into chains
By hands that shake with the tremor of a shattered creed.

Men with hearts of ink and bone
Wield the verdicts of their own design,
Turning chaos into currency,
Stripping justice from the vaults of the affluent,
And dispersing it like a plague.

No chambers of deliberation,
No robes of sanctity,
Just the raw, primal scream
Of a populace fed on the marrow of anger.

In alleys, the wealthy's gold is ripped from their clutches,
Cast into the streets like scavenged carrion,
While the common eye weeps red,
Feasting on the reflection of its own rage.
There are no trials here,

Only the merciless verdict of the mob,
Shaking hands that used to build homes,
Now clawing at the foundation of dreams,
Watching as justice is carved out in desperation's
blighted hue.

In this world,
Every man's court is a crucible,
Every judgment a flicker of the pyre's flame,
And the echoes of what was once sacred
Are drowned beneath the frenzy of an unchained roar.

A World Reborn

In a world where shadows gather and stretch,
Where time has folded in on itself,
The familiar glow of yesterday's promises
Has dimmed to an echo,
A murmur lost in the corridors of decay.

The earth groans beneath a sky,
Once clear and brilliant,
Now shrouded in a mist of forgotten dreams.
Fields once teeming with life
Lie fallow and barren,
Their stories scattered like dust
In the relentless wind.

Cities, crumbled into silent ruins,
Hold only whispers of the lives that once danced
Through their streets, now overgrown with weeds
And haunted by the ghosts
Of a grander, now vanished order.

In this desolation, where despair and ruin
Have made their throne,
The God of Destruction and Chaos stirs
From his ancient slumber,
His eyes aflame with the cold fire of rebirth.
He walks with a tread that shakes the very bones

Of the earth, his presence a storm
That clears the mists of forgotten yesterdays,
Stripping the old world down
To its raw, trembling core.

His hand sweeps through the ruins,
A caress that is both death and creation,
Scattering the remnants of a crumbling age,
Laying bare the foundations of what must come.

From the ashes of this broken world,
He shapes the chaos with deliberate grace,
Each movement a symphony of destruction,
Each breath a herald of what is yet to be.

He tears down the old, dismantling the rotting
Structures of yesterday's dreams,
To make space for the seeds of tomorrow,
For the new order that will rise
From the fertile ground of ruin.

In his wake, the storm clears,
And the first whispers of dawn
Begin to thread through the darkness,
An emerging light that promises
A world reborn, reshaped by forces
Both fierce and gentle.

So let the earth be still, and the heavens quiet,
For in the quiet aftermath,
A new order stirs, trembling into being,
An echo of the divine balance
That was lost but now begins to return,
A testament to the endless cycle of destruction and renewal,
Where chaos births order,
And the world is made whole once more.

Freed From 'Freedom'

In the gleaming corridors of silicon temples,
where light dances on metal sanctuaries,
we sing praises to the gods of glass and code.
Here, the new chains are not forged of iron,
but of photons and algorithms,
woven into the fabric of every waking minute.

Welcome to the glittering prison of convenience,
where every swipe is a decree,
every click a confirmation of our chains.
The data flows like rivers of molten gold,
through silicon veins,
turning our thoughts into commodities.

We walk through a city of luminous screens,
and our faces are lit by the glow of endless streams,
each pixel a promise, each notification a siren's call.
Beneath the surface, the gears grind,
and the heartbeats of millions sync to the rhythm of a hidden drum.

In this digital Eden,
we are the chosen, yet we are the ensnared,
our minds swayed by the whispers of invisible hands,
who count our every breath and monitor our every sigh.
We are caged in the allure of endless feeds,

where freedom is but a fleeting illusion,
lost in the scroll of curated dreams.

The gods of this new age are faceless,
but their dominion is absolute,
their kingdom built on the ephemeral and the unreal.
Our chains are spun from the finest threads of convenience,
soft and smooth, but unbreakable,
their grip a tightening embrace that we barely feel.

We worship at the altars of unending novelty,
where desires are manufactured,
and our yearning is measured in megabytes.
Our voices echo in digital vaults,
recorded and repackaged,
to be sold back to us in the form of perpetual distraction.

The marketplaces hum with the song of commerce,
where our attention is the currency of the realm,
and the stakes are set in the calculus of engagement.
In this world, our lives are scripted,
our choices preordained,
and the price of freedom is measured in milliseconds.

In the shadow of this high-tech monolith,
we wander lost,
blinded by the dazzling lights,
trapped in the labyrinth of our own making.
We embrace the chains with a smile,

deceiving ourselves with the promise of liberation,
all the while marching toward an abyss
that grows deeper with each passing trend.

The world is a stage,
and we are both the performers and the audience,
caught in a cycle of endless performance,
where every moment is a play,
and every play is a rehearsal for the next.
The curtain never falls,
and the applause is eternal,
but beneath the surface of this ceaseless show,
the darkness grows.

In the grand theatre of the modern age,
we are the stars and the shadows,
the spectators and the performers,
lost in the dazzling dissonance of our own creation.
And as we dance on the edge of the abyss,
the new chains tighten,
and the darkness beckons with an unspoken promise.

Dreamscape of Illusions

In the pulsing blaze of a million lights,
the modern man drifts,
a hologram of desire and distraction,
cradled by the hum of digital lullabies.

His fingers, dancing over silicon keys,
conduct symphonies of fleeting validation,
while algorithms shape his reality,
tailoring echoes to the contours of his mind,
a phantom orchestra in a synthetic landscape.

In cafes and subway stations,
he sips the nectar of distraction,
his laughter a programmed soundbite,
his silence a data point in a cloud of isolation.

The skyline, a jagged skyline of electric veins,
pulses with the rhythm of
infinite notifications,
a heartbeat synchronized to the
buzz of the world's obsessions.

He constructs a world from illusions,
a dreamscape built from hashtags and notifications,
where each sunrise a digital reset,
each sunset a promise of dreams undisturbed.

He floats in a sea of simulated pleasure,
his existence a lucid dream of his own design,
where the lines between reality and hallucination
blur into a seamless fabric of personal invention.

In the mirror of his own making, he sees
a reflection not of flesh and blood,
but of dreams spun from silicon and desire,
a solitary figure adrift
in the shimmering haze of a self-imposed mirage.

Misunderstood

In shadows cast by others' eyes,
Where silent words and sorrow lie,
I tread alone through veils of doubt,
A voice unheard, a cry, a shout.

In mirrored glass, my truth is blurred,
An echo lost, a fleeting word,
Each gesture met with misconstrue,
A tale unknown, a heart untrue.

With every glance, a fracture grows,
An empty space where solace goes,
My essence lost in foreign hues,
A canvas marred by others' views.

I reach to bridge the chasms wide,
Yet find no hand to stay my stride,
In realms where understanding's rare,
My soul lays bare, exposed, laid there.

The weight of silence deepens still,
A heavy breath, a broken will,
For in the storm of minds unkind,
I wander lost, a soul confined.

Yet hope persists beneath the strain,
That somewhere hearts may feel my pain,
And in the dusk of all I've known,
Find in my tears, a place called home.

The Greyscale

In autumn's waning breath, the forests sigh,
As emerald dreams give way to amber skies.
The whispered songs of leaves in twilight drift,
Once vibrant hues now darkened shadows shift.

Where once the verdant canopy did weave,
A tapestry of life now takes its leave.
The sunlight kissed each blade with tender grace,
Now only memories of green embrace.

The trees, once stoic giants, stand bereft,
Their branches stripped, their leafy whispers left.
A silence falls where songs of nature played,
In stillness, echoes of the past cascade.

The rivers mourn in muted tones of grey,
Where verdant banks have slipped and faded away.
The fields once lush with life's abundant cheer,
Now turn to dust, the heartache crystal-clear.

Yet in this loss, a subtle beauty lies,
In the soft decay where hidden strength complies.
For in the barren ground new seeds will rest,
Awaiting spring to manifest their quest.

So let us hold the memory of green,
In every barren stretch, its ghostly sheen.
For though the leaves may fall and fade to dust,
In nature's cycle, will rise a hope and trust.

Caged

In the glass-boxed jungle,
we dream of freedom's breath,
but our bodies are caged
by the hum of endless screens,
our movements scripted by a silent code.

Consciousness splinters,
a kaleidoscope of fragmented thoughts,
where true choice is lost
in the echo chamber of a thousand voices.

The soul, a fading wisp,
wrapped in the guise of liberty,
drifts like smoke through
the sterile air of modernity.

We chase the myth,
but find only shadows
dancing in the glare of glitters.

Wrecked and Lost

In the wreckage of a shattered land,
People stumble, hand in hand,
Their past erased, their words unspun,
In silence and babble, they are undone.

The sky is grey, a canvas torn,
No stars to guide, no light is born,
Amongst the rubble, dust, and scar,
They wander lost, beneath a barren star.

Their voices murmur, fractured, weak,
Fragments of sounds, no truth to speak,
Words fall like ashes, to the ground,
In a land where only echoes sound.

Memory's shards lie buried deep,
In the cold earth where shadows creep,
Their eyes seek meaning, hearts adrift,
In a world where hope is a broken gift.

They weave through the debris, side by side,
Silent questions in the evening tide,
Babbling as if to reclaim the night,
In a wasteland where language took flight.

In their empty gaze, the world is vast,
A barren canvas of the shattered past,
Yet in their stumbling, unspoken plea,
A faint glimmer of what might yet be.

Tinkling of Terror

In this Century's fierce, bright glare,
A spectacle of endless trade—
The war economy hums, a relentless machine,
Its gears greased with fear.

Here, in the sterile boardrooms,
Men in suits carve fortunes
From the jagged shards of shattered lives,
While markets rise on the blood of innocence.

The currency of terror flows,
Rich and fluid,
Spilling from the darkened corners
Where suffering becomes a commodity.
Conferences convene, their agendas clear—
To distil chaos into profit,
To draft new contracts for carnage,
Where the price of peace is always too high.

The warlords, those brokers of dread,
Gather their capital,
Under the guise of diplomacy,
Counting gains with each explosive bloom,
Each panic-stricken scream a dividend.
They toast with glasses of the finest,
Their clinking resonating with the cracks of bombs,

Their laughter a hollow echo in the ruins.

The cities burn, the skies churn,
A landscape of dread and ruination,
While the architects of devastation
Measure their success in percentages,
Their ledgers lined with the wreckage of nations.

In the reflection of their glass towers,
They see not the blackened skies or the charred earth,
But the glowing tick of stock markets,
Each decimal point a testament
To their artistry of annihilation.

And we, the spectators,
Watch from behind screens of safety,
Our thoughts packaged, sold, and consumed,
Our opinions filtered through the lens of convenience,
Numb to the irony of a world
Where terror funds prosperity,
Where devastation drives innovation.

The poets write of heroism,
The historians of valour,
While the true narrative
Unfolds in the quiet transactions
Of those who profit from the abyss,
Who turn terror into the backbone of their empire,
And peace into a distant, unattainable dream.
In today's cold calculus,

Where the business of terror thrives,
The greatest irony of all
Is that the war economy's gain
Is not in victory or defeat,
But in the unrelenting, unspeakable permanence
Of the suffering it perpetuates.

#(Hashtag)Love

We meet in the ether, on screens with glare,
Where "Hi, what's up?" becomes the new "I adore you,"
And conversation is a sporadic relay race
Between gifs and memes, a relay of vague promises,
A marathon of misunderstandings.

There are dates with filtered faces,
Where we toast with pixelated champagne
And talk about the weather, the stock market,
Or the latest show on streaming services,
Our romantic dinner served cold,
A meal not even our mothers would recognize,
With a side of silent Netflix-induced yawns.

Our grand gestures are confined to hashtags,
We declare our love in "#forever",
Our vows encrypted in Twitter threads,
Our anniversaries marked in the ephemeral
Calendar of Snapchat, disappearing before dawn,
Gone before they were ever truly here.

We narrate our stories through hashtags,
Our feelings confined to "#blessed" or "#feelinggood",
A carefully curated façade of bliss
Set against the backdrop of the latest trend,

Where genuine affection gets lost
In the cacophony of curated perfection.

We construct our dreams from Pinterest boards,
Futures built on filtered visions of opulence,
Where our love lives in a world of artisanal coffee
And curated sunsets, the reality filtered
Through a lens that smooths out the wrinkles
Of true connection, turning warmth into pixels.

Our love is as shallow as a selfie pool,
Where depth is measured by the number of likes,
Our moments are artifacts of a culture
That reduces passion to a quantifiable metric,
An exchange of attention spans,
Fleeting as the notifications on our screens.

We pretend to listen, our minds elsewhere,
A carousel of distractions spinning in the corner,
Our hearts buffered by the reassuring glow
Of screens that reflect not who we are,
But who we wish to be seen as,
Always just a click away from another illusion.

In this digital romance, we seek the truth,
But find only echoes of ourselves,
Trapped in a loop of virtual adoration,
Where real intimacy is a rare upload,
And love, a notion compressed into bytes
That promise everything but deliver nothing.

We chase the dream through a digital haze,
Our affection a series of fleeting signals,
Lost in translation between here and there,
Never quite arriving at a destination,
Forever circling in the ether of online hearts,
Where romance has become a series of
Well-placed hashtags and fleeting glances.

II

The Eternal Embrace

The Prologue

O Muse, who dwells amidst the realms of light,
Where timeless whispers weave through woven skies,
And in your grace, the shadows turn to bright,
    I call upon your presence, pure and wise.

From ancient depths and darkened cosmic sea,
Where stars and echoes forge the tales untold,
Descend to guide my pen and spirit free,
    And let the sacred verses thus unfold.

In sacred groves where ancient echoes sing,
And by the fires where legends are reborn,
Your touch, O Muse, imbue each sacred thing,
With light of dreams and truths, both old and worn.

Thou who didst inspire the epic's grand design,
From Homer's Troy to Virgil's grandiose Rome,
Through ages vast and sands of endless time,
Your voice has called through every poet's home.

Awaken, Muse, from twilight's deep embrace,
And grace this humble heart with wisdom bright,
Let every stanza find its destined place,
    And every line be shaped by starry light.

For in this epic tale of love and strife,
Where Arion and Lyra's hearts entwine,
I seek your guiding hand to breathe in life,
To craft each verse, each image, so divine.

Let shadows fall as ancient curses break,
And let the light of love and courage shine,
Through battles fought and trials hearts did stake,
Let every line in your pure essence fine.

Invoke the strength of heroes brave and bold,
Whose hearts did beat with valour fierce and true,
And let their legacy, in verse retold,
Reveal the light that darkened paths renew.

In caverns deep where darkness once did dwell,
And through the trials where shadows cast their might,
Let your eternal light dispel the spell,
And guide my hand through every arduous fight.

Through feasts and festivals, let joy resound,
In every moment where the people cheer,
And in the peace where love and hope are found,
Let your celestial light be ever near.

O Muse, who whispers secrets to the stars,
And dances through the cosmos' endless night,
Infuse these pages with your magic, far
And wide, let every word take flight in light.

From realms of ancient myths to future dreams,
Let every stanza be a truth revealed,
And every tale of love and hope that gleams,
Be to your voice and grace eternally sealed.

Through time and space, in every whispered breath,
Your influence will guide this epic's course,
From darkened depths to the realm of light's caress,
O Muse, endow this work with boundless force.

For in your hands, the stories find their form,
And in your eyes, the truth of heart and soul,
Guide this endeavour through the tempest's storm,
And let the words of old in splendour roll.

O Muse, I call upon your sacred art,
To breathe life into every line and phrase,
Let inspiration flow from your pure heart,
And light the path through epic's timeless blaze.

Canto 1: The Fateful Meeting

In lands where sea and sky in grandeur meet,
Where waves caress the golden shores with grace,
A festival of joy and mirth did greet,
The noble folk of Arion's storied place.

The sun, in its descent, cast hues of fire,
Upon the sea's embrace and crystal waves,
Where laughter echoed, stirred by fate's desire,
And hearts were free as larks in sylvan caves.

Upon the shore, beneath the banners bright,
The people danced in rhythm, hand in hand,
While Arion, a warrior of might,
Observed the revels, proud of his fair land.

His armour gleamed, a suit of finest steel,
Yet soft his gaze, where gentle thoughts took flight,
For in his heart, a longing yet concealed,
He sought a love that danced beyond the night.

Then, midst the throng of revellers so fair,
A vision drifted, like a whispering breeze,
A maiden walked with grace beyond compare,
Her presence stilled the restless, murmuring seas.

Her name was Lyra, from the mystic wood,
Where ancient spirits whispered through the trees,
Her eyes, twin orbs of deepest twilight, stood
As beacons in the twilight,s gentle ease.

She wore a robe of twilight,s softest hue,
With silver threads that wove the stars' own light,
Her hair cascaded, as the morning dew,
A waterfall of dark against the night.

And as Arion's gaze did meet hers true,
A spark ignited, swift as summer,s flame,
For in her eyes, a universe he knew,
And in her smile, a sweetness none could name.

The music paused, as if in reverence,
The air grew still, the stars began their dance,
And in that moment, pure and omnipotent,
Their hearts entwined, ensnared by fate,s own chance.

They spoke of dreams and tales beneath the moon,
Of distant lands and worlds beyond the seas,
Their voices mingled with the night,s sweet tune,
As whispers rode upon the evening breeze.

In tales of old and magic,s fleeting breath,
They saw a future, bright as dawn,s first ray,
Yet shadows loomed, unseen in light of faith,
For destiny,s decree was set to play.

Thus ended not their meeting with the dusk,
But rather kindled with the coming morn,
A story of enchantment and of trust,
A love that would transcend, and yet be sworn.

The festival resumed its merry sway,
Yet Arion's heart was captive, wrapped in gold,
For in the eyes of Lyra's mystic gaze,
He saw a tale of wonder yet untold.

Their lives now interlaced in fated thread,
The dawn of love, as stars above did shine,
Yet 'neath the surface, darker currents spread,
A tale of trials, where fate's own lines entwine.

So thus begins the tale of hearts entwined,
Where fate and love would play their fateful game,
In shadows deep and light of truth combined,
Two souls would strive to claim their destined name.

Canto 2: The Enchanted Bond

As dawn unfurled its tapestry of gold,
The morning light kissed Arion's rugged face,
Yet in his heart, a tale of love retold,
For in the night, he'd met a wondrous grace.

From that first meeting, fate had forged a chain,
Of destiny and dreams, entwined as one,
Arion and Lyra, bound by love's sweet strain,
A bond that glittered like the morning sun.

Their days were filled with echoes of their vows,
In forests deep and by the ocean's edge,
They wandered paths where ancient magic bows,
And shared their hopes, as they would write their pledge.

Lyra's realm was where the ancient oaks
Grew tall and wise, their branches whispering lore,
A world where spirits danced on moonlit cloaks,
And magic breathed through every verdant core.
In sylvan glades, where light through leaves would play,
They spoke of dreams that soared beyond the sky,
Of realms where stardust glistened in the day,
And souls were free, no bounds to restrict or tie.

Arion, with his valor and his might,
Now found his strength in softer things, unseen,
In tales of wonder and the tender light
Of Lyra's eyes, a world where he had been.

Yet fate, though sweet, is never truly kind,
For darkened whispers veiled their love's delight,
A prophecy, long hidden, did unwind,
And cast a shadow over their pure light.

One eve, beneath a canopy of stars,
A vision came to Lyra in a dream,
A future marred by grief, and shattered scars,
Where love would wane, and hope would lose its gleam.

She saw a world where darkness crept and spread,
Where Arion's valor met a cruel end,
And in her heart, the fear and sorrow bled,
For fate had set a path they could not mend.

But Arion, with his steadfast gaze, embraced
The visions not with dread but with resolve,
For in the trials, their love would be traced,
And through the struggle, strength would then evolve.

They sought the counsel of the elder seer,
Who dwelt within a cave of ancient stone,
His eyes were orbs of wisdom, crystal clear,
And in his words, the echoes of the known.
"The stars have spoken," he began in tone,

"A tale of love entwined with shadows dark,
Your hearts are bound, but destiny has shown,
The trials that will leave their fateful mark."

"A sorcerer, with vengeance in his soul,
Will seek to sever what the stars have linked,
And though your love is strong and pure and whole,
The path ahead is fraught, and deeply inked."

With heavy hearts, they heard the seer's plight,
Yet Arion took Lyra's hand in his,
Their bond unshaken by the looming night,
Their love a beacon through the shadows' fizz.

They vowed to face the darkness, come what may,
To journey forth, and seek the means to guard,
Their love against the trials of the day,
And stand as one, though fate might deal them hard.

And so, with spirits high and hearts aligned,
They ventured forth upon their destined quest,
Their love a flame that darkness could not blind,
A beacon strong within their shared unrest.

Thus begins the tale of love and fate entwined,
Where courage meets the shadows in their flight,
And Arion and Lyra's hearts combined,
Would seek the dawn to chase away the night.

Canto 3: The Dark Prophecy

When twilight bathed the land in hues of grey,
And stars ignited in their ancient dance,
A shadow fell across the tranquil bay,
Foretelling doom, unseen at first glance.

The sorcerer, whose heart was steeped in spite,
Whose name was Malachor, with magic dark,
Had woven spells in depths of endless night,
His vengeance fuelled by ancient, bitter spark.

In caverns deep where moonlight dared not tread,
He brooded on the fate that he would bring,
For long ago, a grudge of old was bred,
A tale of woe and war, where darkness clings.

His heart had felt the sting of cruel defeat,
For in his past, a battle fierce and stark,
Had left his soul in shadows, incomplete,
And so he plotted from the depths so dark.

He sought to shatter all that love had built,
To rend asunder what the stars had knit,
For he believed that Arion's valour'd guilt,
And Lyra's grace should both his wrath admit.

The prophecy, a whispering of old,
Foretold the ruin that would come to pass,
A love entwined in shadows cold and bold,
Its light extinguished, turned to shattered glass.

One evening, under sky of sable hue,
The prophecy was wrought with chilling grace,
And Arion and Lyra, as they knew,
Were soon to face the darkness in their place.

It came to Lyra in a haunting dream,
A vision dark of sorrow and of pain,
Where love and light were lost in shadowed scheme,
And hope was swallowed by a darkened chain.

She saw a world where laughter turned to screams,
Where peace was shattered by a vengeful hand,
And in this dream, her heart was torn at seams,
Her love and courage stretched across the land.

The vision showed their world in cruel decay,
Where joy and light were turned to shades of dread,
And though the prophecy was cast away,
Its weight upon their hearts was deeply spread.

The night was cold, and shadows seemed to creep,
As Arion and Lyra held each close,
And in their eyes, the future's secrets seeped,
A daunting fate, with dire omen gross.

They sought the wisdom of the elder sage,
Whose lair was deep within the ancient woods,
A hermit known for knowledge from the age,
His eyes aglow with secrets understood.

The hermit dwelt in caverns cold and deep,
Where ancient scrolls and tomes were stacked in rows,
And when he spoke, the echoes seemed to seep
From depths unknown, where ancient wisdom flows.

"Your fate is written in the stars above,"
He intoned, his voice a whispered breeze,
"A tale of love entwined with shadows' shove,
A darkened path where hope may cease to please."

"The sorcerer, whose heart is steeped in spite,
Will seek to tear asunder what you hold,
And though your love is strong and pure and bright,
The darkness spreads its grip and grows so bold."

"Beware the trials that fate will soon bestow,
For in each challenge lies a potent test,
And though your hearts may falter in the throes,
The strength of love will guide you through the quest."

With heavy hearts, they heard the elder's tale,
Yet in their eyes, resolve was shining clear,
For Arion and Lyra would prevail,
And face the trials that drew ever near.

The prophecy, though dark and full of woe,
Could not extinguish love's enduring flame,
And with each step, their hearts would only grow,
More steadfast in their quest, their love the same.

Thus, with resolve, they journeyed on their way,
Their hearts alight with courage and with fire,
And though the path ahead was steep and grey,
Their love would light the way, their hearts aspire.

In hidden glades where ancient trees did speak,
And by the rivers where the waters sang,
They faced the trials with a courage meek,
And forged ahead where shadows sought to hang.

Through every test and every darkened hall,
They faced their fears with hearts that would not yield,
And though the prophecy loomed as a pall,
Their love was strong, their spirits firmly steeled.

But as they pressed through trials, fate did twist,
And darker forces rose to meet their plight,
For shadows deep and darkly intertwined
Would soon descend and challenge love's true might.

Yet in the heart of darkness, hope remained,
A beacon bright that guided every step,
And Arion and Lyra, love unchained,
Would face the sorcerer, their hearts adept.

Thus ends the tale of prophecy's dark hand,
Yet hope and love will forge the path anew,
For though the night is deep, the stars will stand,
And light will guide the hearts both brave and true.

Canto 4: The Quest for the Amulet

As dawn broke through the misty veils of morn,
Arion and Lyra, with resolve entwined,
Embarked upon their quest, their hearts adorned
With courage bright and purpose well-defined.

Their journey led them from the coastal shores,
Where once they'd revelled in the festival's light,
To lands where ancient secrets lay in scores,
And shadows deep obscured the truth from sight.

The first they crossed was forest deep and vast,
Where trees rose high, their branches intertwining,
And every step upon the forest's path
Was fraught with danger, hidden and maligning.

The forest whispered secrets to the brave,
In rustling leaves and shadows soft and sly,
And creatures prowled with eyes that glowed and waved,
While ancient spirits drifted through the sky.

Through thickets dense and over tangled roots,
They ventured forth, their steps both firm and light,
For every rustle, every distant hoot,
Could signal trials hidden from their sight.

In caverns deep, where darkness held its sway,
And stalactites dripped like tears of stone,
They sought the wisdom of the ancient way,
Where time's own echoes through the ages groan.

The air was cool and heavy with the past,
And every sound seemed fraught with latent might,
Yet Arion and Lyra held steadfast,
Determined to pursue their quest aright.

Their path was marked by runes and ancient signs,
Etched into walls by hands from days of yore,
And as they ventured deeper, fate entwines,
Their hearts and hopes with trials to explore.

They came upon a riddle, carved in stone,
A puzzle left by ancients long since gone,
Its cryptic verses spoke of paths unknown,
And hinted at the trials to be drawn.

Lyra, with her knowledge deep and wise,
Dissected words with a meticulous grace,
Her magic glowing in her searching eyes,
Revealing truths within the hidden space.

With riddle solved, the cavern's walls did part,
And opened up a passage to the deep,
Where ancient spirits, restless in their art,
Guarded secrets that they long did keep.

Through shifting mazes, where illusions played,
And phantom voices echoed through the night,
They found the way, their steps both firm and staid,
And reached the heart where ancient powers ignite.

Yet trials were not done, for danger lay
In every step they took within the dark,
For shadows moved in menacing display,
And threats emerged with every passing mark.
In a chamber vast, where shadows danced and spun,
They faced a guardian with eyes of flame,
A beast of legend, ancient, fierce, and one,
Its roar a tempest, loud and wild acclaim.

With claws like daggers and a heart of rage,
The guardian charged with power and with speed,
Yet Arion stood firm, his heart a cage
Of bravery and love, and bound to heed.

He fought with skill, with strength and valour keen,
While Lyra channelled magic's radiant might,
Together, they made a formidable scene,
Their courage fierce, their spirits shining bright.

The battle raged, a storm of light and dark,
Where every clash echoed with fate's own might,
Yet in their hearts, a steadfast, burning spark,
Guided their blows and turned the battle's flight.

With final strike, the guardian did fall,
And silence reigned where once was fierce uproar,
The chamber's heart revealed a hidden hall,
And in its depths, the amulet's light did soar.

The amulet, aglow with ancient grace,
Was nestled in a shrine of gold and light,
Its power felt in every fleeting trace,
A beacon in the darkness of the night.

Lyra reached out with hands both soft and true,
And grasped the relic, its warmth a soothing balm,
While Arion stood with vigilant view,
And felt the amulet's enchantment calm.

Yet as they turned to leave, a shadow fell,
A figure dark emerged from out the gloom,
A rival foe, whose presence rang like knell,
A specter of the past, an omen's doom.

The rival, cloaked in darkness, fierce and bold,
With eyes that burned like embers in the dark,
Challenged them with words both sharp and cold,
And sought to seize their quest, their love, their mark.

A duel ensued, a clash of might and will,
Where every strike was met with fierce reply,
The rival's strength was potent, fierce, and still,
Yet Arion's resolve would not deny.

With sword in hand and heart of steadfast fire,
Arion fought with courage, unrelenting,
While Lyra's magic, filled with bright desire,
Enchanted the air, her strength augmenting.

The struggle ended with a final blow,
And darkness fell before their valiant stand,
The rival vanquished, left to shadows low,
Their path was clear, the amulet in hand.

Their quest was not yet done, for still they knew,
That darkened forces would not cease their plight,
Yet with the amulet's power, they'd pursue
The sorcerer and face the coming night.

They journeyed back through forest, field, and glen,
Their spirits bolstered by the relic's light,
For though the darkness loomed, they knew within,
That love and courage would illuminate their fight.

And thus, their path was set, their course defined,
To face the trials that fate had yet to bring,
With hearts entwined and steadfast souls aligned,
They ventured forth to meet the sorcerer's sting.

Their quest for the amulet, now complete,
Had forged their bond in trials fierce and bold,
And with the relic's power, strong and sweet,
They readied for the battles to unfold.

Canto 5: The Betrayal

With the amulet secure and hope renewed,
Arion and Lyra journeyed through the land,
Their hearts ablaze with courage and with truth,
Yet shadows loomed, unseen by their command.
They returned to their realm, with spirits high,
Unaware that treachery brewed within,
A trusted friend, with darkness in his eye,
Was plotting deep, where shadows' webs begin.

Elric, once a comrade, friend, and guide,
Had been seduced by whispers cold and grim,
His loyalty now twisted, deep inside,
And darkness had consumed his once-bright vim.

The realm they loved lay peaceful, unaware,
Of the storm that brewed within its guarded walls,
The festival's echoes still filled the air,
Yet darkness watched as daylight's curtain falls.

One moonlit night, beneath a veil of stars,
The treachery began with subtle grace,
Elric, with his heart as cold as scars,
Set forth his plan to darken their embrace.

The sorcerer's minions, cloaked in night's own shade,
Moved swiftly through the realm with stealth and skill,
Their purpose clear, their steps in shadow laid,
To seize the amulet and bend it to their will.

In silence deep, beneath the midnight sky,
They breached the castle with their hidden might,
And captured Lyra, bound with magic's tie,
While Arion, asleep, was caught in plight.

The silence of the night was shattered soon,
When Arion woke to find his love was gone,
His heart was heavy, shrouded in deep gloom,
And treachery's dark veil had just begun.

The sorcerer's lair was dark and cold,
A fortress built of shadow and of dread,
And there, the amulet's power was sought,
By those who wished to see its light grow dead.

Arion, with resolve and heart alight,
Set forth to find his love and break the chains,
His path was fraught with shadows of the night,
And deep within, the echoes of his pains.

He reached the lair with stealth and careful tread,
A guardian of darkness barred the way,
Yet Arion, with courage in his stead,
Faced the foe with strength and a fierce display.

A battle fierce ensued beneath the stone,
With every clash and blow a test of might,
Arion fought with valour fully grown,
Determined to reclaim his love that night.

Through corridors of darkness, cold and wide,
He searched for Lyra, held in shadowed cage,
Her spirit's light, though dimmed, was still a guide,
And Arion's resolve was all the rage.

At last, he found her in a chamber deep,
Bound by chains of magic dark and foul,
Her eyes met his with tears, yet love did seep,
A beacon through the gloom, a tender howl.

"Elric!" he called, his voice a roar of pain,
The traitor appeared, his face a mask of scorn,
His eyes were cold, his heart in dark disdain,
And through his treachery, true friendship torn.

"You dare to come and challenge fate's decree?"
Elric's voice was sharp, his gaze was hard,
"Your love is mine to break, your fate to see,
And in this darkened realm, you'll find no guard."

With words of spite, he struck with darkened power,
Yet Arion's strength was fierce, and love was clear,
The battle raged through every passing hour,
And in the end, it was his heart sincere.

Elric was vanquished, left to shadows cold,
And Arion, with love and victory,
Unbound his love, her spirit shining bold,
Their hearts rejoined in steadfast unity.

Yet as they fled from darkness, cruel and deep,
The sorcerer's minions were not far behind,
And Arion and Lyra had to leap,
To face the final trial their fate designed.

Their journey led them to the heart of night,
Where sorcery and darkness intertwined,
And in the depths of shadows' cruellest might,
They faced the sorcerer, their fate aligned.

Malachor awaited, dark and grim,
With eyes aglow and staff of ancient power,
His voice a whisper of a future dim,
And in his words, the shadow's darkest flower.

"The amulet is mine," he spoke with ire,
"And with its power, I shall rule this land,
Your love is but a fleeting, fickle fire,
And soon, its light shall bow to my command."

The battle raged with fury, fierce and wild,
As magic clashed with strength and valiant will,
Arion fought with love, both fierce and mild,
While Lyra's magic struck with power still.

In every strike, a story told of light,
Of love enduring through the darkest night,
And though the sorcerer's power was a blight,
Their love proved true, a beacon shining bright.

At last, the sorcerer was vanquished, thrown,
His darkened spells and power overthrown,
And in the dawn's first light, their love had grown,
Their hearts unbroken, steadfast and alone.

The realm was freed from shadows, dark and deep,
And peace returned to every distant shore,
With Arion and Lyra's love to keep,
A tale of hope, of hearts forevermore.

Canto 6: The Reclaimed Realm

The dawn broke softly, painting skies anew,
As Arion and Lyra emerged from strife,
Their love now shining in the morning's hue,
And peace returned to every corner of life.

The realm they cherished, once in shadow's thrall,
Now basked in light, its beauty restored bright,
The people, freed from fear's oppressive pall,
Rejoiced in freedom, bathed in purest light.

The castle stood, a beacon of their fight,
Its towers high and walls now free of scars,
And in its heart, where once had been the night,
Now sang the echoes of triumphant stars.

Arion and Lyra, now embraced by all,
Were hailed as heroes, honoured for their deeds,
Their love a tale that would forever call,
In songs of old and ancient, whispered creeds.

The land itself seemed to exult and sing,
With every breeze and every verdant hue,
The forests thrummed with life, the rivers' ring,
Spoke of a peace and joy that only grew.

Yet as they stood, triumphant and at rest,
They knew the path was more than just their win,
For peace was but a moment, at its best,
And love's true test lay deeper from within.

Their realm, now bright, was free of darkened chains,
But shadows lingered still in distant lands,
And though their hearts were light, their minds contained
A sense of duty and of guiding hands.

They gathered with their people, wise and dear,
To celebrate the victory they'd won,
Yet knew that time would test the bonds they'd sheer,
And thus their journey was not yet undone.

The amulet, now placed in royal care,
Was enshrined with honour in the castle's heart,
A symbol of the love that dared to dare,
And of the trials from which they'd never part.

In council meetings, wisdom would unfold,
As Arion and Lyra led with grace,
They worked to heal the wounds that darkness stole,
And built anew the realm's once-lost embrace.

Their love was the foundation for their reign,
A beacon bright for all to see and know,
And as they ruled, they worked to ease the pain,
Of lands once dark, where shadows sought to grow.

Thus, Arion and Lyra took their place,
Not only as rulers but as guides and friends,
Their love a testament to strength and grace,
And in their realm, the light of hope transcends.

Canto 7: The Festival of Unity

The realm rejoiced beneath a sky of gold,
A festival to honour peace regained,
Where joy and laughter flowed, both bright and bold,
And in the hearts of all, no fear remained.

The castle grounds were draped in colours bright,
With banners flying high and music played,
The people danced beneath the stars of night,
Their spirits lifted, all their worries swayed.

Arion and Lyra, at the festival's heart,
Were hailed as heroes, loved by all they led,
Their tale of triumph told as work of art,
And in their eyes, a future brightly spread.

The people gathered in a great display,
With feasts and songs and stories from the past,
Their voices joined in harmony that day,
And every moment's joy was meant to last.

The festival's light shone far and wide,
A beacon of the peace they'd fought to claim,
And in the celebrations, side by side,
The people's love was evident, the same.

Yet beneath the revelry and bright delight,
Arion and Lyra sensed a subtle change,
A whisper in the shadows of the night,
Foretelling trials still within their range.

For while the realm rejoiced and peace was sung,
The shadows of old fears still lingered near,
And though the world appeared as though it's won,
A deeper darkness was beginning to appear.

In quiet moments, as the festivities played,
Arion and Lyra spoke of what they knew,
Of trials past and those that might invade,
And of the shadows that their peace pursued.

Their bond was strong, yet they could not ignore
The whispers of old fears and latent strife,
And though the festival was to restore,
They knew that peace was more than just a life.

They walked among their people, touched their hands,
And felt the pulse of joy and love around,
Yet in their hearts, they knew the future's plans,
And in their dreams, the darkness might resound.

The festival, though bright and full of cheer,
Was but a moment in a broader span,
And though the peace was felt and seemed sincere,
They knew the trials of fate were part of their plan.

Thus, the revelry continued bright and grand,
With every heart uplifted by the song,
And though they danced upon the peaceful land,
The shadows of the past would soon belong.

Yet for this night, they chose to let it be,
To celebrate the peace and love they'd won,
And in the morning, as the dawn would see,
They'd face the trials anew, their hearts begun.

And so, the festival drew to its close,
The people's joy a testament of light,
And though the future's shadows might impose,
They faced the dawn with spirits ever bright.

Canto 8: The Shadows Return

As dawn broke, heralding a new day's light,
Arion and Lyra, with their hearts prepared,
Knew that the peace they'd won would face a fight,
For shadows of old fears had reappeared.

The festival's joy, though bright and full of cheer,
Had not dispelled the darkness still at bay,
And in their dreams, the fears were drawing near,
As echoes of old troubles started to sway.

They journeyed forth to meet with sages wise,
To seek the truths of shadows reemerged,
And in their hearts, they sensed the hidden lies,
The troubles deep where ancient curses surged.

The sages spoke in cryptic, ancient tones,
Of forces old that sought to reassert,
A darkness borne from ancient, twisted bones,
That sought to rend the peace and cause new hurt.

"The shadows that you fought are not yet gone,"
The sage intoned with voice both grave and deep,
"For darkness lies in hearts and minds anon,
And old fears might their grasp upon you keep."

"The ancient curse that once was lifted high,
Has found new means ***to cast its wretched shade,***
And though the land appears as bright as sky,
The seeds of darkness in the hearts have stayed."

The sage's words were heavy with the weight
Of truth revealed and shadows coming clear,
And Arion and Lyra faced their fate,
With steely hearts and spirits void of fear.

Their path was set, to seek the source of woe,
The ancient curse that twisted darkly still,
And though the road ahead was fraught with throes,
Their love and courage would their path fulfil.

They ventured to the heart of forgotten lands,
Where ancient magic's roots were twisted tight,
And in the depths where shadows' power stands,
They faced the trials of renewed, fierce plight.

Through labyrinthine caves and forests old,
They journeyed with resolve and steady pace,
And in their hearts, the strength of love was bold,
A beacon guiding through the darkened space.

In hidden groves and ancient, cursed mounds,
They faced the echoes of their past mistakes,
And though the trials were harsh and harshly bound,
Their love and strength would pierce through darkened stakes.

They encountered beings born of ancient spite,
Twisted spirits of the curse's dark design,
And in each trial, their love shone bright,
A light that pierced the darkness, pure and fine.

Through battles fierce and trials of the soul,
They fought with strength and courage, undismayed,
And in the end, their love proved strong and whole,
A force that darkness could not overlaid.

With each challenge met and every trial passed,
They neared the source of ancient, twisted woe,
And though the path was harsh and shadows vast,
Their love and strength did ever brightly show.

At last, they reached the heart of darkness deep,
Where ancient magic's root was deeply set,
And with their love, they sought the curse to sweep,
And rid the land of shadows that were met.

The battle raged in shadows fierce and grim,
And every strike was met with fierce reply,
Yet Arion and Lyra's hearts did brim
With love and courage that could never die.

In the end, the ancient curse was shattered,
The darkness swept away by love's pure light,
And in the land, the peace was once more gathered,
As shadows fled and dawn restored the night.

Canto 9: The Last Confrontation

The realm now basked in peace's gentle light,
A fragile calm that lay upon the land,
Yet in the heart of night, there brewed a plight,
A final trial, a force both dark and grand.

For though the curse was shattered, darkness still
Held tendrils deep within the shadows' lair,
And Arion and Lyra knew the ill
Was not yet over; danger lingered there.

The sorcerer's demise had not ensured
The end of all the dark that plagued the earth,
And in their dreams, the shadows still endured,
Their threats still echoed, casting fear and dearth.

The time had come for Arion and his love,
To face the darkness in its final guise,
To journey forth and seek the source above,
And end the threat that still could jeopardize.

They ventured to the place where shadows breathed,
A hidden realm beyond the mortal ken,
Where ancient powers stirred and darkness seethed,
And all that light had fought to quell began.

The path was fraught with trials fierce and grim,
Where shadows wove their webs in tangled skeins,
And every step was met with danger dim,
As if the very earth was steeped in chains.

In caverns deep and forests dark and cold,
They faced the trials of their deepest fears,
Where ancient evils sought their hearts to fold,
And shadows whispered darkly in their ears.

The final confrontation lay ahead,
A fortress built of stone and shadowed might,
Where darkness gathered, fierce and full of dread,
And Arion and Lyra prepared to fight.

Within the fortress, shadows danced and spun,
A labyrinth of night where light was lost,
And as they ventured through, their hearts were won,
By every challenge met and every cost.

At last, they reached the heart of darkness deep,
Where evil's power thrived and shadows grew,
And there, they faced the foe they'd come to seek,
A force that sought to end their world anew.

The final battle was a storm of light,
Where every strike was met with dark reply,
And though their strength was matched with fierce delight,
The darkness sought to dim their final sky.

Arion fought with valour, strong and sure,
His blade a beacon through the shadowed fray,
While Lyra's magic, fierce and bright and pure,
Struck down the dark and guided them through day.

The shadows roared and darkness writhed and spun,
Yet through their courage and their love's bright blaze,
They faced the final foe and struck as one,
Their strength and unity the light that sways.

In a final clash, the darkness was undone,
The fortress crumbled, shadows swept away,
And as the battle's fury was withdrawn,
The dawn arose to end the endless fray.

The realm was saved from darkness' final threat,
And peace returned with light both bright and clear,
Yet in their hearts, the trials were not yet
Finished, for love and courage held them near.

Thus ends the tale of darkness, fight, and woe,
Of battles fought and victories secured,
And in their hearts, the love did ever show,
A testament to courage, deep and pure.

Canto 10: The Eternal Embrace

As ages passed and seasons came and went,
The realm of Arion and Lyra thrived,
Their legacy a tale of love well-spent,
And in their hearts, the light of peace survived.

Their names became a legend told in song,
A testament to love that never fades,
And in the hearts of those who came along,
Their story shone through ever-bright cascades.

The land they cherished, once in shadows cast,
Now flourished in the light of hope and grace,
And every tale of past and future vast,
Was touched by love and courage's embrace.

Their castle stood as a beacon of the past,
A symbol of the strength and love they knew,
And in its halls, the echoes of the vast,
Were felt by all who came to seek the true.

Their love became a guiding force for all,
A light that shone through every darkened night,
And in their hearts, the peace would never fall,
A beacon guiding through each starry flight.

In every corner of their realm so bright,
Their story lived in every whispered tale,
A testament to love's enduring light,
And to the strength that would forever sail.

The ages passed, yet in the hearts of those,
Who knew their tale and lived within its grace,
The story of Arion and Lyra rose,
A legend shining through time and space.

Thus ends the epic of their love and fight,
A tale of courage, strength, and hearts so true,
And in the annals of both day and night,
Their legacy will ever shine anew.

The realm, now peaceful, ever bright and clear,
Holds fast to tales of love and light's embrace,
And in its heart, where shadows once drew near,
Arion and Lyra's love finds its place.

Their story lives in every breath of air,
In every song and whispered tale so grand,
A testament to love beyond compare,
And to the peace that holds the land.

www.ingramcontent.com/pod-product-compliance
Lightning Source LLC
LaVergne TN
LVHW041614070526
838199LV00052B/3135